# FOOD & FOLK

Book design and photography (except where indicated)
by Leif Södergren

Cover:
Photo Leif Södergren
Olga and Folke Jonsson's dining room at Lysholmen, Särö

Back cover:
Photo Leif Södergren
From a tea and coffee shop in Gothenburg

Illustrations:
Drawing on opposite page,
and other drawings on p.40, 60, 61 and 64.
by Donovan O'Malley


ISBN  978-91-982015-6-7


**LEMONGULCHBOOKS**
www.lemongulchbooks.com

# FOOD & FOLK

LEIF SÖDERGREN

Donovan O'Malley

# CONTENTS

Donovan O'Malley

# INTRODUCTION

Much of human activity is centered around food. We think of food whether we're hungry or not. We spend a great deal of time buying it. We take hours preparing it (well, some do). We talk about it. We read about it in cook books. We watch television when chefs talk about it (sometimes to excess). When we socialize, it is often centered around the communal intake of it. We give it as gifts. Food, we can't escape it!

Memories are often connected to the smell of a certain food. The sense of smell (the olfactory system), an important survival mechanism for primitive man, has a direct access to the brain so we instantly recognize a particular smell. That is why a smell, pleasant or unpleasant, can bring back a memory in a flash. In this book however, memories have been brought back (fairly fast) by searching among old photos. The result is a series of memories and thoughts on food and those who cooked it, going back many decades.

Some people become keenly interested in preparing food for themselves and others; many have become what we call "good cooks". Usually a degree of creativity is involved together with a keen interest to entertain and a need to take care of others, to be a good host. It is such people that one remembers, and that is how I got started on Food & Folk, remembering, for example that excellent couple, Beatrice and Clayburn La Force on their ranch in Alpine California. After that I just kept going.

# CALIFORNIA

To be invited to Sky Mesa Ranch was an event. One was not only served excellent food, the entire house and all around it was a personal museum of the people who lived there and was a treat to behold. The couple, Beatrice and Clayburn La Force, had met in San Diego in 1923 and built their charming rustic home in 1949 in log cabin style from old redwood (termite safe) railroad ties, cement blocks and native stone.

Clayburn, an investment banker in San Diego, loved the genre of the old West and collected western artifacts. There were wagons scattered all over the plateau (mesa) surrounding their home and spurs and branding irons hung on the outside of their house.

Inside it was highly personal and full of interesting things collected by this creative couple. The La Forces lived surrounded by many animals, two Arabian horses, one donkey, doves, ducks, cats, a dog and two geese. The nights here were still and the sound of coyotes could be heard and Bea wrote in a local newspaper that she had once heard the forlorn, incredibly sad wail of one of the last mountain lions, sad because the mountain lion was mourning for the loss of her species.

It's hard to believe, but Beatrice and Clayburn La Force's vegetable and fruit garden, two thousand feet up in the hills of Alpine outside San Diego, had once been sea bottom. The soil was enormously fertile.

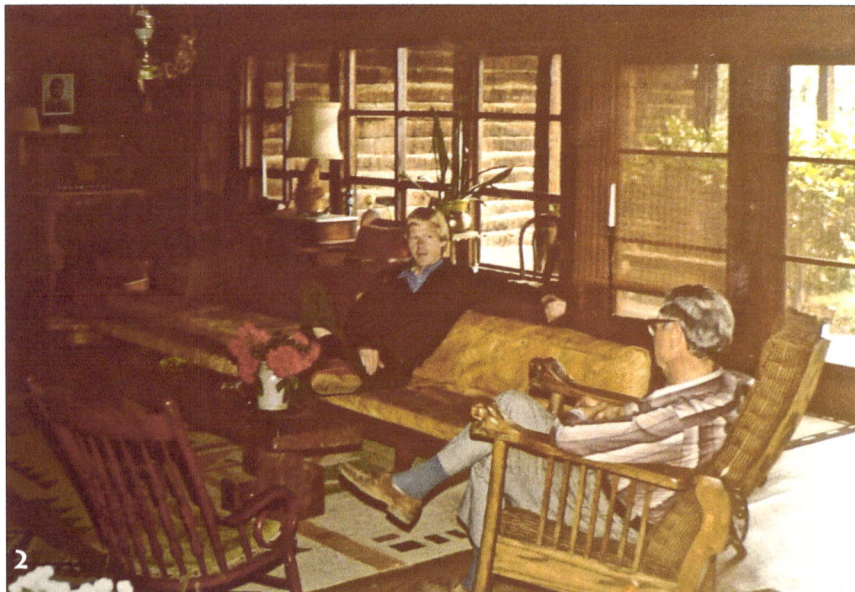

1. The house they built by rail road ties 1949.
2. The living room with home-made furniture.
3. The back of the house - the courtyard.
4. Beatrice (Bea) and Clayburn La Force 1979.
5 Fireplace built by local stones.
6. Bea and Donovan O'Malley 1979.

1. Leif (the author) helps to put up bean posts in 1975. The soil (former sea bed) was very fertile and succulent figs and fragrant grapes flourished beside all traditional vegetables. There were also orange, lemon, peach, plum and nectarine trees. With such fine produce one could make the splendid 'Alpine Orange Peach Conserve' (Recipe on p. 9).

2. The rustic Old West-style house was built with redwood rail road ties and rocks from the ground nearby.

3. The kitchen with many artifacts, including Swedish Folk Art painted by the author.

4. As you approached Sky Mesa Ranch you saw all the wagons, this was indeed an outdoor museum.

## BEATRICE LA FORCE'S ZUCCHINI RELISH

Sometimes zucchinis can get away from you and grow enormous in a very short time. This is how Bea used them. As she suggests below, you can use less sugar if you wish. I would recommend to cut the sugar in half (2.5 cups). It is nice to see her handwriting.

Here's what's cookin' Zuccini Relish — makes approx ~~serves~~ 3 qts

Recipe from the kitchen of Bea L.

10 cups of ground zuccini
4 " " " onion
2 green peppers
1 red (or green chili) pepper
4 tablespoons of salt
grind zuccini and onion, add salt and let stand over night - next day rinse well in cold water, drain well - add ground peppers and the following = (over)

5 cups of sugar (you can use less, to taste)
2½ cups cider vinegar
1 tablespoon dry mustard
1 " " tumeric
2 " " Corn starch -

Cook about 30 minutes - Stir gently occasionally - Seal at once in hot sterile jars.

**Above:** Bea La Force (1905-2002), was engaged in many community and civic organizations. She and her husband started the Alpine Historical Society. She worked for the local newspaper and the Alpine library.

She invited local schoolchildren when they studied Alpine history and showed them how people in the Old West lived. She demonstrated how to cook on a wood stove and grind corn for tortillas and many more things involved with the past.*

**Left:** The Viejas (old) mountain, 4187 feet, could be seen in the distance from Sky Mesa ranch. Such a majestic mountain with its shifting moods from hour to hour, and season to season, inevitably affects the people who live around it, whether or not they are aware of it, Bea wrote in one of her **"Intimate Glimpses"** in the 'Alpine Echo', a few of them included in her much acclaimed book: **ALPINE: History of a Mountain Settlement 1971** -- available from The Alpine Historical Society.

*Source: The Alpine Sun Shopper March 5, 2009

## A CABIN IN THE WILD

In this charming little cabin (above) on Sky Mesa Ranch which Bea and Clayburn graciously loaned to me and Donovan for a time, I baked the best corn bread ever. Bea supplied fresh ground corn and whole grain wheat from their grinder up at the main house. The wonderful dry hot air, the utter peace and the donkey Becky and the two Arabian horses looking through the kitchen window, made the eating of the corn bread all the more pleasurable.

When you move into a cabin that has not been occupied for a long time, you must be prepared to share it with the previous inhabitants. A huge black widow spider presided, strategically placed, in the window. Stink bugs and small scorpions walked across the floor, and mice appeared, unafraid (in Disney fashion), from everywhere eating the crumbs that fell to the floor as we ate our food. But (in 1975) when a rattle snake menaced us just outside our door, Clayburn's shotgun came in handy (right).

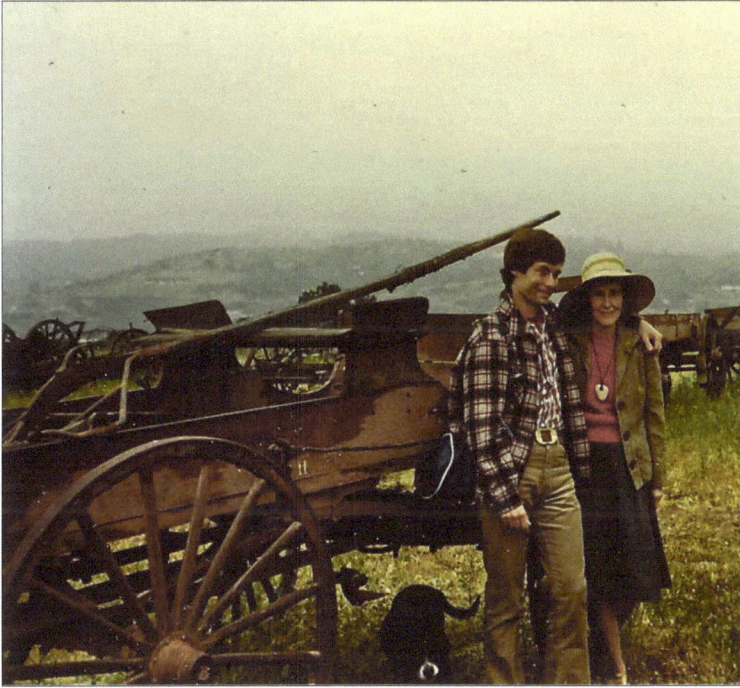

**Above:** Bea was a writer of plays and books and a local historian. She had her own writing "shack" as she called it. She once wrote to me about two mockingbirds arguing for some nest outside her shack: *"Opera was never so divine"*. Here she is with the author (above left) and fellow writer Donovan O'Malley in 1979 (top right) by the collection of wagons on the adobe mesa.

**Left:** A rare lily, the Chocolate Bell (Fritillaria lanceolata), grew on the adobe mesa. Walks on the mesa were enchanting, especially in the evenings when the weather had cooled off. It was fun to look for trap door spiders that lurked in their holes below ground, waiting beneath a trap door for an insect to walk by. Sensing the vibrations of the passing insect, the spiders opened the trap door and shot out dragging the insect back into their round, silk-lined hole. Quite a show.

**Below:** It was always something fun to do or discover at Sky Mesa Ranch. Like talking to the donkey, Becky - as Donovan is attempting below.

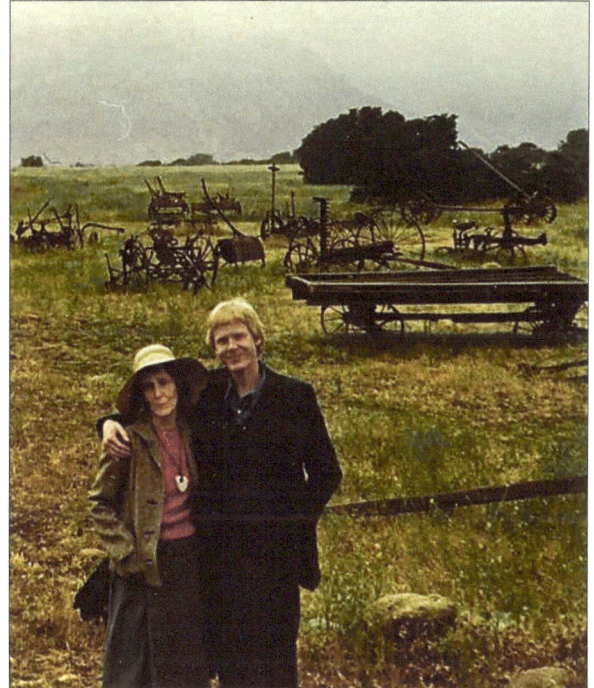

## ALPINE ORANGE PEACH CONSERVE

A wonderful recipe if you have sun ripened fruit from your own trees.

INGREDIENTS:
3 oranges, 1 lemon (organically grown)
5 cups or three lbs peeled and diced peaches
1.5 cups golden or dark raisins
8 cups sugar
1 cup coarsley chopped walnuts
1/2 cup drained maraschino cherries

Wash and dry the oranges and lemon, then quarter them. Remove seeds and put trough a food chopper using the coarse blade.
Into a large kettle add: the citrus fruit, peaches and raisins. Add sugar, stirring occasionally until sugar dissolves. Bring to a boil.
Reduce heat and simmer until mixture sheets from a spoon or a candy thermometer registers 221 degrees Fahrenheit, (105 C) about 1 hour. Stir in walnuts and cherries. Ladle into hot sterilized jars and seal.

**Above:** Clayburn (1) stands before an enormous cactus. It is good protection against fires, the constant threat in this dry land. The Alpine climate is hot and dry and considered a healthy climate for those with respiratory problems. The little rain in spring brings grass and shrubs to life and the balmy air smells of wild grass and blossoming shrubs.

Note the 'cactus apples' or 'prickly pears' that can be carefully picked and eaten. But special protection and treatment is needed to guard against the spikes. In Mexico, the tender shoots of the cactus are used for cooking and also cattle feed. Cactus candy and cactus juice is also common.

**Above**: Bea loved animals, the wild ones out there, and all the domestic ones they kept, including the doves above. I'm not quite sure why the doves were kept, but the rattle snakes had feasted on quite a few of them judging from the feathers outside their nest situated only a few feet from our cabin.

**Left**: The goose (3) that each night was lovingly taken into the kitchen where newspapers had been placed on the floor. This was necessary to protect it from coyotes or skunks. The goose in return fiercely protected Bea. Their dog Igor sometimes got in a tangle with skunks and Bea had to wash him in tomato juice to rid him of the intense skunk smell.

**Far left**: Bea talks to their donkey, Becky while Leif, the author, watches. In the background is one of their two Arabian horses (2).

## SKY MESA ORANGE ZEST POWDER

The orange trees seen behind the pigeons were grown without pesticides so the thin peels could be used for dried orange zest. We were welcome to take as many as we wanted.

Before squeezing them for juice, I peeled off the orange peel with a potato peeler and let the peelings dry. When I had collected a quite a lot of these thin dried curly orange peels, I ground them in a blender into a fine powder and used it to season our tea.

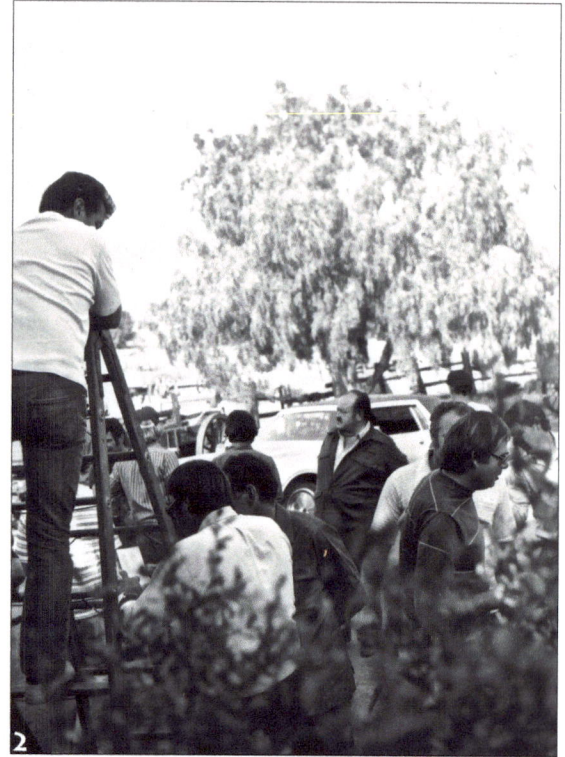

## FILMING "CANNON" ON SKY MESA

It was quite a surprise to find the rural idyll of Sky Mesa Ranch filled with film trucks and crew early one morning. We had not been told, but Bea and Clayburn had allowed the filming of one of the weekly episodes of the television series "Cannon" (1971-76). The star of "Cannon" was William Conrad (1920-1994). He played the overweight private detective with a fondness for fine foods. (1-5).

We were invited to eat whatever we wanted from the restaurant truck that served the film crew. That day we had breakfast, lunch and dinner from their canteen and what a splendid Chili Con Carne they had. Everyone in America has their own recipe for "Chili" and I wouldn't dare to offer mine.

The next day all was quiet again. The silence was welcome, but we missed the food truck and all the free food served directly outside our cabin door.

4. The noted film and stage actor, Ralph Meeker, speaks to Donovan O'Malley during an intermission of the filming in the living room of Sky Mesa Ranch.

5. William Conrad, the star in Cannon, talking to the director.

7. One of the many western wagons on Sky Mesa Ranch.

6 and 8. Two "locals" (Leif and Donovan) posing on western artifacts, maybe hoping for an offer as an extra by the film company?

**Above:** For Clayburn, who liked to collect western artifacts, the flat adobe mesa was the perfect exhibition area for all the wagons he collected over the years. The dry weather and little rainfall meant that the wagons did not deteriorate outdoors.

Clayburn and Bea had held on to their ranch despite the steep property taxes in San Diego. They bought the 260 acres homestead in 1946 and finished the house they built themselves with redwood rail road ties, by 1949. They and their many visitors enjoyed the openness of the large ranch. In the mid 1970s, it was unique with so much land when most properties in the vicinity consisted of much smaller lots.

**Left:** Old cattle branding irons, spurs, horse shoes, horse bits, and western memorabilia hung on the walls on the outside of the house facing the courtyard. Note the visible rail road ties used to build the house (in sizes of 8, 12 and 16 feet, held together by mortar).

**All above:** The enormous bed bought in an estate sale was so tall that a special room had to be constructed (the outside of the room can be seen on p. 4) and soon this large space was filled with more items.

But people who stayed here claimed they experienced a ghost in the room, something to do with the bed and its previous mysterious owner. But there were more things to contend with. Like insects.

When you were a guest in this house you had to roll with the punches and not panic if a hairy tarantula spider the size of your hand walked across the floor. These spiders never worried Bea and Clayburn. The insects might look scary but their bite was no worse than a flea bite unlike their poisonous and deadly South American cousins. But some people might not enjoy the crunching sound when, on the way to the bathroom in the middle of the night, one accidentally stepped on a large hairy spider.

## SKY MESA RANCH FONDLY REMEMBERED

As I nostalgically view the old photos from a time when Bea and Clayburn lived at their beloved Sky Mesa Ranch, I feel enriched to have experienced their grand hospitality and to have such fine memories of them and their enormously interesting home.

With the aid of internet real estate listings in Alpine, I can amazingly see the new houses built where the ranch once stood. I recognize the hills, they are the same, but the new houses with arched windows, chandeliers and marble floors have been planned on a drawing board far away and have not been built in the organic way Bea and Clayburn went about creating their home, a home that once delighted and fascinated so many.

But then, originality can never be reproduced.

When I first looked at the house plans of the small house we built in 1971 on a lot in San Diego, I was surprised at the small kitchen. It looked like a tiny closet. But Donovan reassured me by building a cardboard model of the house. We looked at all the rooms, peeking through the window openings from various angels and were convinced that this would indeed be small, but would work for us.

The house fit between a massive pepper tree, a huge Haas avocado tree and a cup-of-gold vine that wound in and out of the tree top. Large cup-of-gold flowers with the fragrance of pineapple and coconut bloomed abundantly. Ferns from the edge of the property grew up into the low hanging limbs, creating a wall of green in every direction. A cantilevered balcony jutted right into all this greenery. A tree house!

A contractor built the two story eighteen feet square frame, attached the exterior cladding and installed plumbing and electricity. The rest was up to us, to finish: exterior paint, interior plasterboard and the cabinets in the little kitchen.

This was a small, efficient, very practical kitchen with a fold-up work counter. In this small space I made more good food than anytime in my life, and we had a minimum of china and bowls. My mother had given me a basic cook book from Sweden (Vår Kokbok) and it proved invaluable since I had never cooked to any greater extent. I tried all sorts of foods I remembered having eaten and liked in Sweden.

I surprised our friends with a variety of tortes such as Mocha Torte, Princess Torte, and Sacher Torte. It was all great fun. People were surprised that I did everything "from scratch", but how can you start cooking using cake mixes? They seemed to have rather a lot of preservatives as well which did not appeal to me.

During the six years I stayed in California, it became a tradition that I had a "Swedish Smörgåsbord" on the twenty-third of December. Funny how things can suddenly become a tradition.

We had many guests and I cooked many dinners and every dinner, I took a plate of the main dish and the dessert to Donovan's grandmother Vera, "Ma", who lived next door. Being of pioneer stock, she never overindulged in words and she gave the exact response to every dish: "Pretty rich". When I asked for more details, the response was always: "Pretty rich". No more no less. Ever. But she loved it.

photo: Ricardo H. Martinez

photos: Ricardo H. Martinez

Photo from family archives

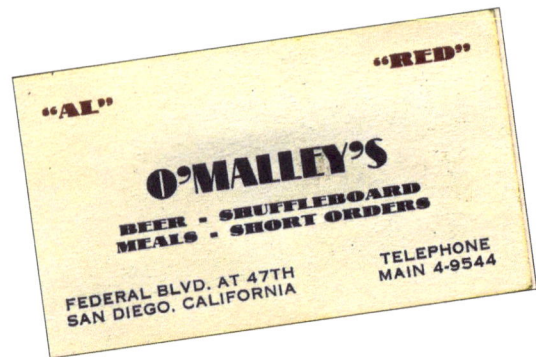

"AL" "RED"

## O'MALLEY'S
### BEER · SHUFFLEBOARD
### MEALS · SHORT ORDERS

FEDERAL BLVD. AT 47TH
SAN DIEGO, CALIFORNIA

TELEPHONE
MAIN 4-9544

Grandmother Vera, "Ma" (Donovan's paternal grandmother), lived next door to us in San Diego. Ma and her husband Albert, always referred to as "Big Dad", had experienced two depressions and their story was not dissimilar from the Joad family's in John Steinbeck's novel "Grapes of Wrath". Having left Kansas during one depression, moving to Oregon, they later left for San Diego, looking for jobs during another depression in the 1930s.

Donovan lived with them during WW2 and food was heavily rationed so Ma kept chickens on an empty lot next door that they owned. Donovan learned how to gut and clean the chickens. Some chickens were sold but the family always had chicken on Sunday.

On Wednesdays, Ma, Big Dad and Donovan had corn bread for dinner. It was eaten with milk and sugar in a bowl and was very popular with young Donovan as there were not so many dishes to do. Sometimes they took the car downtown to park and simply "watch people go by". Pleasures were simpler then.

Many years later, during the mid 1970s when we lived next door, I used to eat lunch with Ma when I was at home from my studies. I always enjoyed our lunches. She used to fix all sorts of quick little dishes that she had learned during her many jobs in various restaurants. She had been head pastry chef at Morgan's Cafeteria in San Diego. When her son, the boxer Red O'Malley opened up "O'Malleys" she served a set lunch every day ("short orders"). Whatever she fixed was always completely sold out. There was a jukebox at "O'Malleys" and Ma who couldn't dance asked her grandson Donovan to teach her to dance which he happily did.

Ma was sharp, highly principled and always advanced to a management position, whether in a canning factory, or clerking estate auctions or at Ryan Aeronautical during the WW 2.

# BEAUTIFUL MOTHER MARIAN

Boxes of preserves used to arrive regularly to us in San Diego from Marian, Donovan's mother who lived in the fertile San Joaquin Valley in central California. Marian found great joy in picking and preserving the fine produce available up there. She loved sharing everything with friends and relatives. Marian made her "Bread and Butter Pickles" with Armenian cucumbers. When sliced, they had fluted edges, very decorative. She managed to get them crisp by adding salt and ice for three hours before starting the pickling. She added some bell peppers and onions and seasoned with cloves, turmeric and mustard seeds and equal amounts of vinegar and sugar.

She knew many of the local farm families and she was allowed to pick whatever was left behind after the harvest. She also had her own garden and grew okra, tomatoes, grapes, figs and much more.

Once when we visited her in the valley, the bottom drawer of her fridge was full of chilled freshly picked cantaloupes that were superbly fragrant and sweet. Whatever is shipped to Sweden is picked green so it was nice to have tasted the real thing at its height.

From a farm nearby she bought pomegranate juice and made pomegranate jelly, another discovery in one of her surprise shipments she dispatched to us in San Diego. Wonderful with my homemade scones.

The very beautiful mother Marian loved growing the food, preserving or pickling it and then giving it away, a nice combination that delighted us and many others.

1. Marian working at Ryan Aeronautical during WW 2. She was considered the most beautiful woman there.

2. Donovan and parents before a Maersk vessel (ca 1941), bound for New York from Panama.

The American flag painted on its side is to keep German submarines from torpedoing the vessel as it passed through the Carribbean. The U.S had not yet joined the war.

3. Marian in later years, still beautiful. She moved to Sweden where she spent 17 years.

Photos from family archives

- 19 -

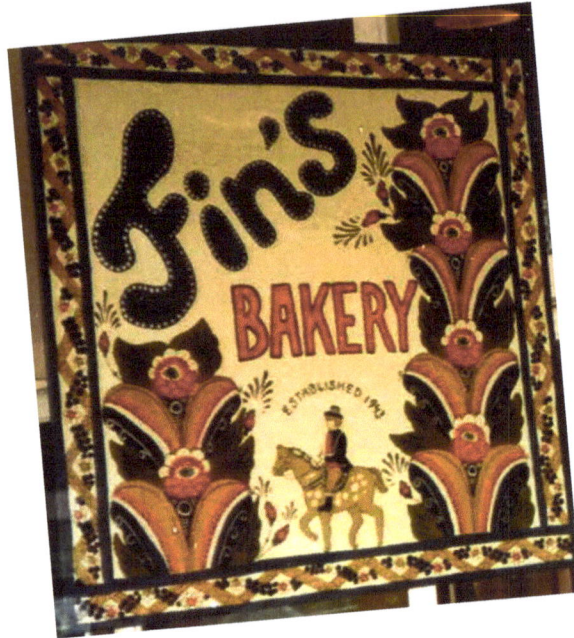

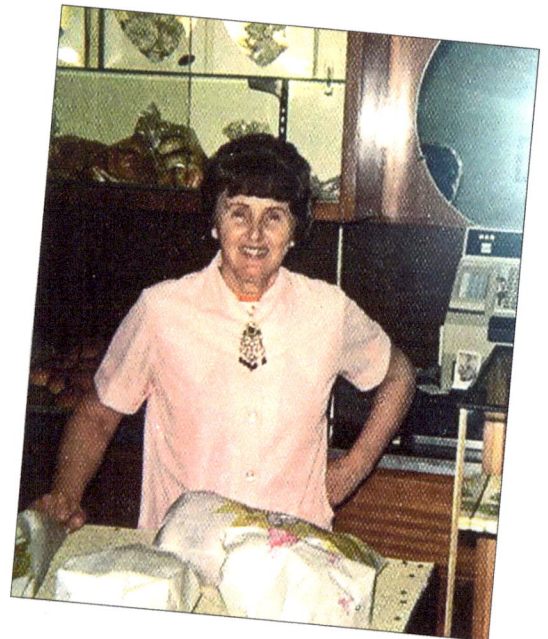

Suddenly one day, in the early 1970s, the long abandoned bakery (in the Golden Hill district of San Diego) had new tenants. It was a hard working Norwegian couple, Ruth and Fin Andersen who, near retirement, had decided to make a fresh start on the West coast by taking over the abandoned bakery once called 'Parker's Pastry Palace'. They probably did not know that Golden Hill which was at its height during the nineteen-forties was now declining. But finding an empty bakery was not easy.

Fin did all the baking himself and Ruth, with her sing-song Norwegian accent and always jolly, managed the counter. It was nice to meet some fellow Scandinavians. They came from Utah where they said they had run into difficulties for not being Mormons. But Fin was a fantastic baker with a fine line of bakery goods, he surely would attract a clientele in good time.

Since I was painting and selling Swedish Folk Art in San Diego, I offered to make some signs (for free) to help their business. They would then sell some of my paintings from the shop. They were very pleased. Donovan wrote an article about the fine new bakery in the prestigious San Diego Magazine where he worked. This attention got them many wealthy customers who drove for miles to buy Fin's superb bakery goods. Ruth and Fin couldn't have been more pleased. Their business flourished and eventually they could retire comfortably. It was a sunshine story.

Right: I saw two existing hooks outside the bakery and created a sign (left) that could easily be wired in place. This and some other signs gave the bakery a Scandinavian look. I enjoyed helping them.

Whenever we went in to the shop, a grateful Rut showered us with goodies.

Below:
After leaving California, we kept in contact with Fin and Ruth. They were able to sell their business for a good sum and retire comfortably.

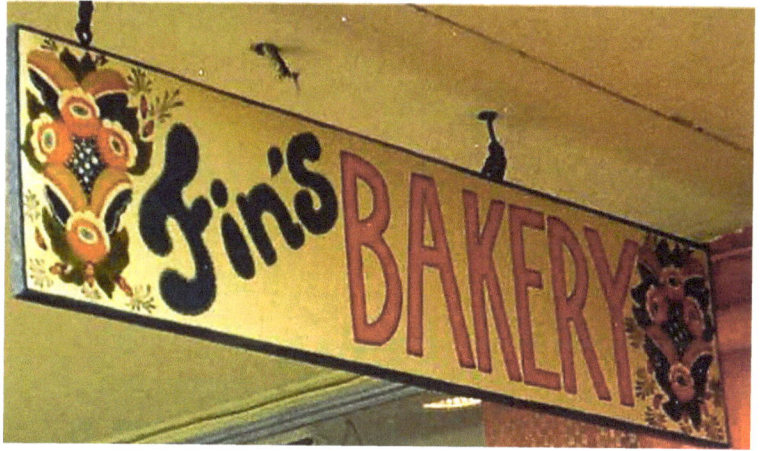

Photo from family archives

# SWEDEN

They were a good team, the three of them; my American grandmother Olga married to my Swedish grandfather Folke and their cook and housekeeper Linnéa. Together they worked wonders in the areas of hospitality and culinary heights.

The cook Linnéa Bertilsson was forty when she left her native Falkenberg for Särö on the coast outside Gothenburg. Everyone in Sweden knew of Särö, the exclusive seaside resort where the Swedish king Gustaf V spent the summers playing tennis and visiting prominent families. Little did Linnéa know during the train ride to Särö, that she would soon be cooking for the king and become his absolute favourite.

Linnéa was locally a very well known cook and was always busy with cooking for large parties. But the Second World War which was in its second year had brought food rationing. To buy food, ration coupons were needed and that made cooking for large parties difficult and sometimes impossible. This could have been the reason for Linnéa taking on this temporary job.

The chemistry between Linnéa and her new employers, Olga and Folke Jonsson seemed to work splendidly and the temporary job became a lifetime dedication. She stayed with them as long as they both lived, and guaranteed in their later days, that they both could live a life that very few of their generation could enjoy.

Food was not rationed at Lysholmen, the home of Olga and Folke Jonsson. Folke hunted and loved fishing and the forests were full of mushrooms and berries. The vegetable garden at the large villa Lysholmen was extensive and there was a large greenhouse and many chickens and ducks. Linneás creativity in the kitchen was by no means stifled by the war. This was a house full of activity and her employers Olga and Folke were creative, generous and great fun to work for.

Swedish King Gustaf V

Photo: Svenska folket genom tiderna

There are some homes when you just feel so absolutely welcome. My grandparents Olga(3) and Folke(4) had such a home (5). Their door was wide open for their friends and relatives. No one ever went away from their home without being beautifully fed. And the person that had a lot to do with that generosity was the nearly super-human Linnéa (1). Photos from family archives

It must have been a thrill to cook for the Swedish king and Linnéa no doubt enjoyed the challenge. It was no secret that the king loved Linnea's food. She was the best cook ever, and he said he couldn't get any better food in his own palace in Stockholm. A local paper wrote that "the king always kept a fresh supply of sweet crisp rolls (socker-skorpor) baked by the cook at Lysholmen".

It was a big event when the king came to dinner. There were locals in the garden peeking in through the windows. The king was very fond of the small shrimp (tångräkor) that were found in kelp at the water's edge ("baltic prawn", palaemon adspersus). Olga and Folke's children (6) used to catch these shrimps with hand-held dip nets where they swam. The day the king was expected, all the children sat down and with their little fingers shelled these miniscule shrimps until they got an enormous plate of these delicacies. Linnéa used to make a special seafood mayonnaise to go with the shrimps.

## LINNÉA'S ROYAL MAYONNAISE

### INGREDIENTS:

One egg yolk
Half a teaspoon table mustard or Dijon mustard
2 teaspoons red wine vinegar
Dash of salt
Dash of white pepper
One cup (2 dl) sunflower, corn or canola oil (room temperature)
Half peeled yellow onion

### HOW TO:

1. In a narrow bowl mix together egg yolk, mustard, red wine vinegar, salt and pepper using an electric beater. All should be room temperature.

2. In a small, steady stream, very slowly pour the oil into the mixture whilst the beater is running full power. Linnéa used to use a wooden spoon, stirring for a very long time, but this is a modern quicker way.

(The beating causes an emulsion which is the mayonnaise. If there is a problem and the mayonnaise separates, get a new bowl and start with an egg yolk. Gradually add the separated mixture to the egg yolk in the new bowl.)

3. Add half a peeled yellow onion and leave it in the mayonnaise. Keep cold. Use within one week. Very good with seafood and fish.

5  Lysholmen, Särö

6  Photos from family archives

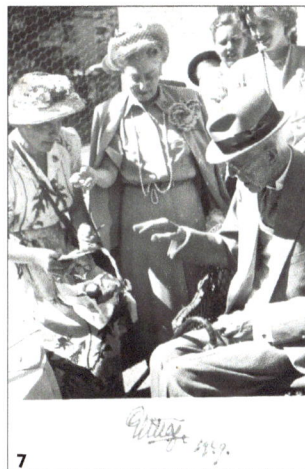

7

1. Linnéa, the wonderful cook.

2. The Swedish king Gustaf V who loved Linnéa's food.

3-4. Folke and Olga

5. "Lysholmen", Olga and Folke's home at Särö, on the West coast of Sweden

6. Olga and Folke's children by the waterside where they would swim and play all summer long. They caught the small shrimp that hid in the kelp, using dip nets. Then they all helped to shell them for the king.

7. Olga and the Swedish King Gustaf V, at a Red Cross bazaar c. 1940.

Photo from family archives

When we brought a guest to mother Gunilla, there was always a nice spread. Before dinner, with drinks, she served a variety of different small sandwiches with seafood, and other delicacies beautifully assembled and displayed on newly polished silver and elegant china. She made it all seem effortless, she was the perfect hostess.

Some people just love to take care of other people, to make them feel good and mother was just such a person. When she and her husband Ulf were the head of a local Italian Association (Ulf had a sister in Italy so they had an interest in Italy) mother made La Sagne for all seventy members of the association It was made in batches and kept in the freezer and served at the annual meeting. So why did she do this while simultaneously working a full time job as a sales rep? She said that she loved seeing the old ladies in the association happy. That was her motivation and her reward.

# GUNILLA'S PRIZE WINNING MIMOSA EGGS

## GUNILLA'S MIMOSA EGGS

1. Cut six hard boiled eggs in half and put on a plate.

2. Put half the egg yolks in a bowl with three tablespoons or more mayonnaise, a dash of salt to taste and a teaspoon or less curry powder. Mash and mix with a fork. It should not be too dry.

3. Divide mixture in empty egg halves using a teaspoon.

4. Use a spoon to press the remaining egg yolks through a sieve over the filled egg halves. They get the "mimosa" look.

5. Garnish and powder with some curry powder if you wish. Sometimes mother put a shrimp on top and a dill sprig.

A kitchen doesn't have to look like an operating theatre with everything white and all surfaces bare. Well that's what I think anyway. No minimalism for me please!

## BAKE YOUR OWN BREAD

There is nothing better than the smell of newly baked bread. Yes, actually, there is something better - the *taste* of fresh baked bread with plenty of butter on top.

Once you get the hang of baking bread, it's very easy. I know a large family where all the husbands in the family are bread makers (no, not bread winners, bread makers).

I favour organically grown grain and a lot of roughage. The health guru Adelle Davis has pointed out that plants grown with artificial fertilizers, do not absorb the nutrients that organically grown plants do. I include bran, linseed and other roughage to make the bread march through the gut like a happily determined 'drum and fife band' (Over-refined white bread tends to become lethargic gut-glue). Roughage also benefits the germs in the gut that act as our immune defence (but that is another story).

**MY BREAD** (all ingredients organically grown)
10 cups white flour, 10 cups coarse wheat (graham) flour
1 cup wheat bran, 1 cup oat bran,
1 cup cracked oats, 1 cup linseeds
3 tablesp. salt and 4 packets dry yeast
Add enough lukewarm water to make a nice elastic dough (Better sticky than dry!)
Knead and let rise in the bowl. Then knead again and divide into baking pans. Let rise in pans under cloth.
Bake in medium oven (225C /425 F). When finished brush with melted butter and water. Cool in towels.

I suppose many of us long for a piece of land to grow something of our own. It is a need, perhaps, that goes back to our early beginnings.

Many of the immigrants that have come to Sweden have started their lives here in an apartment but in their homelands they often had their own house and garden. When they were offered small allotments by the local governments here in Sweden, they performed miracles on these plots. This strong longing for land of ones own is touching.

At work I was given a lot of interesting vegetables from one of the immigrant cleaners who had two allotments where her family grew vegetables. I tried growing some beans from her country, she said that these were the best beans ever, and she was right. But the frost came before they had fully developed. Summers in some parts of Sweden can be short.

It is hard work to prepare the soil, hauling manure, planting and constant weeding. But the pleasure of seeing seeds sprout and flourish, it's worth it. A constant vigilance against weeds is an absolute must. I always used two sticks and a string and planted the seeds below the straight string. Then I could do early preventive hoeing around the strings. Otherwise it is hard to tell the difference between sprouting seeds and sprouting weeds. Photos from the small farm we bought in 1981.

## GIFTS FROM SOUTH AMERICA

It might be a bit cheeky to try to grow vegetables native to South America on the same latitude as Alaska and Siberia where Sweden is situated. Well, you can get away with it if you avoid being exposed to the killer number one: frost. Potatoes, squash and beans are all from South America and very sensitive to frost.

In Sweden it can get really warm in mid April and by then the sun will have warmed up the ground to place the potatoes in the ground (+8C/46 F). But in June, when the potatoes have come up and look proud and perky, we can still get some nights with frost, so certain precautions have to be taken or we risk losing them altogether. As seen above, the potatoes and the runner beans (under the tepees) are doing very nicely under the white material which is removed when the risk of frost is gone. It lets rain through, keeps insects out and acts sort of like a green house.

Beans and squash (and dahlia flowers) that grow late into fall are destroyed after the first frost and even if the frost does not come back and the days are mild, it is over for our dear friends from South America.

# NEW POTATOES : THE BEST THING IN THE WORLD

New potatoes, fresh from the ground are the best food in the world. Fresh cooked and eaten with butter. Simply delicious! I wouldn't miss it for the world! When I could not plant them one year, I thought this was close to a catastrophe. How could one possibly live without them?! It sounds silly, but that's how I felt. Now I have learned to live without them. I buy organically grown potatoes and they have real flavour and are a more than reasonable substitute.

During the month of March and April, I put special planting-potatoes on trays in a cool light room so they would develop stubby green shoots. That gave them an early start in the ground. There are many varieties of potatoes with charming names like Silla, Bellona, Inova, Cherie and Minerva.

Sigurd, our neighbour always brought manure which was placed with the potatoes in the furrows, either hand-dug or made with a tractor.

The next job was to scoop dirt up around the green growth that came up from the potato. It prevented the potatoes from getting green and inedible. Also it resulted in more potatoes as the plant developed more roots.

Most Swedes cook (boil) their new potatoes with dill, but I steam my potatoes, using no dill. They taste splendid the way they are.

1987: Australian play producer Keith Richards, American playwright Donovan O'Malley and British designer Angela Dougall are assisting in planting Swedish potatoes. They place a potato and some manure (from the wheelbarrow) in the furrows which a kind neighbour farmer had ploughed.

It is wonderful to have a garden of one's own but if everything gets ripe at the same time it can become a logistic problem, picking and finding a use for all the produce.

One year the apple tree had so many apples that it was hard to give them away. I made some apple sauce and brought bags of apples (left) to people at work and stored some in the attic only to find out later that we had provided the mice with winter food.

Elks love apples. At night elks came to feast on the apples on the ground (their smacking woke us up), bending their front legs to get close to the ground. Elks that indulge in apples often end up drunk when the apples ferment in their stomach and elks can be seen reeling about intoxicated.

The over abundance of produce and the guilt of seeing it spoil, lead me to do a lot of preserves that I could never use and finally I scaled down my endeavours to suit us and our friends and relatives.

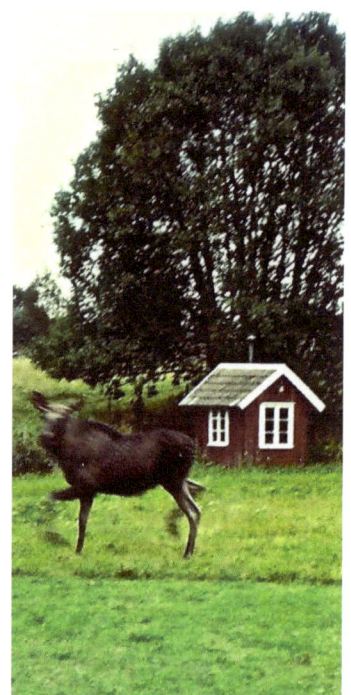

- 34 -

When I started growing zucchini and squash in Sweden early 1980, very few Swedes knew what these strange things were, especially the large, heavy ones that had grown enormous between visits to the country. I gave them away to somewhat reluctant but adventurous friends, with a translated recipe for "Zucchini Relish" (p.7).

I bought many different kinds. The button squash seed sent to me from America, did very nicely and some of them grew as large as a plate size flying saucer. Spaghetti squash was also something fun to try.

The perfect place to grow squash or zucchini is in an old compost. There are a lot of nutrients and it is porous, just right for the fast growing plants to go rollicking about, ending up the size of piglets if you are not there to pick them in time. It really is a growing extravaganza .

Alice and Sigurd, our closest neighbours on the small farm next door, always preferred boiled coffee. Most Swedes brew their coffee these days, but some (10 %) hold on to the old tradition of boiling their coffee, mainly people in the countryside and Northern Sweden. It looks thin but has a nice deep flavour quite different from other coffee.

To make boiled coffee, you put coarsely ground coffee beans with cold water in a coffee pot on the stove. When it all comes to a boil, you take the pot off the heat and let it stand so the coffee grounds sink to the bottom. You can add egg shells (or some cold water) to "clarify" the coffee. Some people have their special tricks for the clarifying process, adding an element of mystery to this process.

In the country, a generation back, people invited each other for afternoon "coffee". Many still do. That was the way people visited one another, dinner parties per se were not so common. These were special events where you dressed up and the hostess had baked her finest bakery goods.

People had to be told by the hostess to start eating and she might say, "Please go ahead and dunk". It did not actually mean that people would dunk (maybe they did at home). The rule was to start with the sponge cake and sweet bread, the "rough dunking" (grovdoppat). Polite people never started with the hard (and more expensive) small cookies baked with cream, butter and sugar and flavourings. There had to be at least seven varieties of those dry cookies, no more no less. If the hostess had baked less than seven she might be labelled lazy. If she had baked more than seven, she might be thought of as bragging (see opposite page for a sample of cookies).

There was also a ritual of pleading and urging the coy resistors who had every intention of tasting everything but could not be seen as greedy or gluttonous. When people had been urged a number of times (some needed three pleadings) and when they had eaten as much as they could, an elaborate cream torte appeared. Some time after that fruit and candy and soft drinks were served and some sweet wine (for the ladies) and brandy for the men. The hostess sometimes offered the guests some of her bakery goods in a napkin. There might be children at home eagerly waiting for a treat.

**Above**: Alice had a great integrity, a sweet nature and was kind, caring and self effacing. She was widowed at seventy-five and after that we grew closer as she became increasingly frail. It was always nice to have an informal cup of coffee with her.

**Left**: In Sweden we have had a very long tradition of drinking coffee from a saucer. In fact, it started with the upper classes. I have seen it a few times, but it is not common anymore. The hot, usually boiled coffee is poured on to the saucer which is deftly and by some, elegantly, held with three fingers. One or two sugar cubes are put between the lips and the coffee is sipped/slurped passing through the sugar cubes (not the modern that dissolve easily). Maybe not the most pleasant to watch or listen to, but it has been quite common and popular in the past.

Coarse ground for boiled coffee.
(2.5 tablespoons to one cup of water)

Medium ground for brewing coffee

Fine ground for espresso coffee

**Above**: It was polite to start with the "rough dunking" (grovdoppa) and then start with the obligatory seven kinds of dry cookies (sju sorters kakor). Today people tend not to eat so many sweets. They still meet for coffee, but they offer different things.

**Above**: At the special coffee invitations, people in the country used the finest delicate china cups to serve the boiled coffee in. Being used to mugs myself, these small super thin cups made me really uneasy. But if farmers with their rough hands could handle them, so should I.

1. Sigurd on the tractor with neighbour Jan who lived on a small farm farther down the road.

Our neighbours, Alice and Sigurd were both in their late seventies but when they had been younger, Sigurd worked at a regular job and was a part time farmer. Alice had taken care of the milking and other chores on the small farm. Now they had only chickens and Sigurd raised calves.

Their situation was similar to the other small farms that lay grouped together in the forest. The stone walls around the fields contained the numerous rocks that had painstakingly been removed from the ground by previous generations. That back-breaking job had fostered hardy individuals.

Most farmers had only three cows, some chickens and maybe a pig. The women milked the cows and hauled the heavy metal milk containers to the road where they hoisted them up on to the raised milk table, ready to be picked up by the diary truck twice a day. Strong women!

2. A very small Alice at 74, is seen at the bottom of the field raking the hay together. This was a labour intensive method of cutting and bringing home the hay. In the past, if there were young children at home they helped their parents bring the hay in. How they must have longed to go swimming with their friends. But that had to wait for the evening. The taking in of the hay was essential.

3. All the women on the small farms kept milking utensils spick and span and this dedication resulted in certificates of cleanliness like this diploma from the dairy.

**Left:** Sigurd had every reason to look pleased that day; he had stacked all his hay in haystacks (with some help from his son Åke who had taken time from his office job) in the fields. The wooden stakes were all hand-made and the wire strung between them was done in a very special way for the hay to dry properly. Hopefully the dry and sunny weather would continue so Sigurd could get his hay home nice and dry. He needed it for the calves he raised (4).

Sigurd kept up this old traditional method of haymaking until the mid 1980s. Alice helped him do some hand raking in the field (left) They were both reasonably old by then. I was amazed at their stamina. I remember lying on the sofa one summer wearing shorts exhausted by the heat. But out in the field, with thick blue overalls in the blazing sun, was Sigurd (over eighty years old) getting his hay into hay stacks!

# "FIKA" : THE SWEDISH ART OF TAKING A BREAK

"Fika" is a Swedish institution; the habit of slowing down with a cup of coffee or tea and something to nibble on. People in Scandinavia drink more coffee than anyone in the world. Whether you are at home or at work, this is an important social ritual covered even by union contracts. Management often joins their employees in this important time of the day. Fika is a must - twice a day.

1. There are many charming places in "Haga" and downtown Gothenburg (4) to fika at.

2. "Two for Fika" drawing by Donovan O'Malley.

3. These ladies have found a perfect spot to fika among the roses in The Garden Society of Gothenburg.

5 Bräutigam's was for many years the finest café with a pianist entertaining the often elegant audience. Unfortunately, only the ornate gilded sign is left.

6. If you want to have a nice fika at home there are speciality shops with personal service to buy the best tea and coffee. You can "sample" the fragrance before you buy (see p. 58).

Above: Things change, these days, daddies on 'paternity leave' often meet downtown for a fika with their children.

This was our favourite café almost thirty years ago, and the reason was the wonderful spirit by those who worked there. Anna and her sister Karin (right) funny and lovingly caring, prepared the best coffee (café au lait served in thick stoneware bowls was the fashion then). The home-made bread and soups were delicious. **Above**: Anna preparing something nice. Today Anna works as a teacher. Karin manages a government department.

**Above:** The café is situated in the charming part of Gothenburg, called Haga. This area was once threatened by total demolition. The city had bought most of the properties, had stopped any building after 1930, and was determined to rebuild with modern houses. Many of the city officials who had themselves grown up here in overcrowded and unsanitary flats, were determined to see these houses torn down.

But others wanted to save Haga. They did not want the kind of modern, nondescript houses that were being built far away from central Gothenburg in "new" areas. The protests became very strong, and in the 1970's the city relented. Haga would not be razed. Many houses were beyond repair, but were replaced by replicas or buildings that fit in nicely with the rest. Today the flats have been made bigger with all modern conveniences. It is now a popular place to live and visit.

Above: Fisherman Knut Karlsson on the island of Rörö, a windswept and sparsely populated island farthest out in the extensive archipelago west of Gothenburg. Below is his daughter Ewy (around 1950), who when she was sixteen, left the island and came to take care of me and my sisters in the city. We loved Ewy, who despite her youth, commanded enormous respect.

When she went home to Rörö, she often brought one or two of us children with her and it was an adventure to stay out there. So much was different from the life in the city. The food consisted mainly of fish and potatoes with maybe meat on weekends.

Knut Karlsson was captain and part owner of this small wooden fishing vessel **GG 192 Roiny**, a long way from the modern vessels used today.

The fishermen needed working clothes and until the 1930's people out here were self sufficient in this respect. There were no shops. Using their own wool, they weaved and made the cloth, from underwear to water-proof outer protective wear, which was impregnated several times with linseed oil.

There was no refrigeration on board, so they brought thin hard bread that had been made at home in the wood fired oven ( see how it was made p.46). On board the rocking fishing boat, the hard bread was soaked in a large sturdy mugs of coffee. When Knut had boiled coffee at home, he preferred really small and thin coffee cups.

During World War II, the population of Rörö witnessed one particularly fierce battle between the British and the Germans not far from their island. The fishermen went out later to look for survivors but in vain. Many of the dead they found are buried on an adjacent island, Öckerö.

**Planting potatoes at Rörö ca 1953:**

Above is fisherman Knut Karlsson and daughter Ewy with my sister who has been given the honour of placing the potatoes in the furrows.

Since the family lived so near the waterfront, they collected kelp to fertilize the ground. Kelp is the perfect fertilizer and has many important minerals, vitamins, proteins and natural plant growth hormones.

The island is comparatively barren and the houses are all perched on granite polished smooth by ice age glaciers (see above). Luckily, not far from the house, there was a patch of sandy soil, perfect for planting potatoes. Boiled potatoes have for generations of Swedes been an essential part of their diet.

I love this picture, frozen in time. Knut, known by all as a very kind man, has been dead for many years and Ewy is over 80, but here they stand, Ewy young and strong and her father healthy and happy to have a little visitor from Gothenburg.

Right: The Karlsson family in 1947, Ewy in white on her confirmation (Lutheran) day. This was two years before Ewy went to Gothenburg to work for us. The young girl had a good hand with children and we loved and respected her enormously.

Photos courtesy of Ewy Karlsson

- 45 -

# BAKING "RÖRÖ FLAT HARDBREAD" THE OLD WAY

It is a busy day (early 1960s) in Ewy's aunt Blenda's special "baking cottage" (bakstuga) on the Swedish island of Rörö. Many family members are involved in the baking of the traditional flat hardbread that the fishermen bring with them on their long trips. They need a lot!

Ewy's father, fisherman Knut, (above) chops wood for the wood fired oven and he generally assists his two sisters today.

**1.** Blenda has a roaring fire going in the wood fired oven. It takes hours to get the right temperature. She needs good dry birch wood for the best result.

2. The dough has been set by Blenda (green dress) and her sister Viola.

3. Blenda is now busy dividing the dough into small round balls (ämnen).

4. Knut's eldest daughter Kajsa (below), uses a rolling pin to flatten the smaller pieces of dough. She places them on special wooden racks (lavar) seen behind her. There the bread rests on pieces of stiff paper, waiting to be put on a round board (fjöl), ready for the oven.

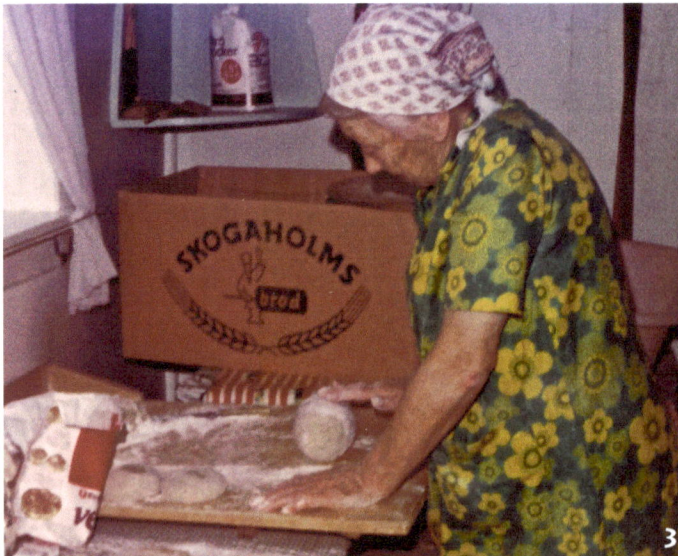

Photos courtesy of Ewy Karlsson

5

**KAJSA'S RÖRÖ HARDBREAD:**
1 kg wheat flour (2.20 lb US weight)
0.5 kg coarse rye flour (1.10 lb)
1.25 dl sugar ( 1 cup or less)
salt and half a packet yeast (1-2 tablesp.)
1.25 hekto margarine (3/4 cup)
8dl water (3.38 cups)
Whole anis and fennel seeds

Let the dough rise for an hour
Divide into smaller balls
Roll out thin
Put in oven on high heat
(or preferably an old wood fired oven)

6

The oven has a wide opening and the fire can be seen inside. Each bread is placed on a metal pan deep inside the oven using a long handled tool. This is a hard and demanding job in front of the hot fire. Blenda and her sister Viola are very busy as they quickly and deftly take the bread in and out (the flat bread bakes very fast), carefully watching that the bread has just the right colour and of course, does not burn.

5. Blenda is working hard. An unbaked bread on a board (fjöl) is on her right.

6. Viola is assisted by brother Knut who hands her the next piece ready to be baked. Afterwards they will all relax with a nice cup of (boiled) coffee and fresh baked bread and butter. A nice social affair.

# ENGLAND

## BETTY MARSDEN ENTERTAINS ON THE THAMES

The enormous, massive round table (left) seated up to fourteen people and was the centre of actress Betty Marsden's magnificent entertainment on the Thames in London. Around this huge round table (this was the case when size really did matter), all the guests could participate and build a really smashing party.

Betty, known as the master of a thousand voices, had everyone laughing just as she had kept everyone in Britain laughing during the 1960's in the radio comedy, "Round the Horn". She was now, in the 1980's, an equally popular stage and television actress, taking her mastery of comedy to new heights on the stage and TV.

She lived on what was a converted coal barge, but in fact it was a very large home with a huge living and dining room and several bedrooms below.

A gangplank led to Betty Marsden's houseboat "THE CHILHAM". A visiting doctor from South Africa, attending a doctor's conference, saw Betty with guests inside with drinks and thought this might be a pub. He walked in and not skipping a beat, Betty asked him in for a drink and we all had a jolly talk until he left for his conference. It must have been a nice memory for him. We certainly had a good time.

1. Kew bridge in the distance seen from THE CHILHAM.

2 . Betty and friends Leif, Beasley and Donovan (Photo F.B Leffew)

3. Betty on one of her visits to Sweden with Donovan O'Malley.

## QUICK MAGIC DESSERT IN CAMDEN

Amazingly, Angela in the middle of renovating her London Mews house was always the most gracious host and excellent cook. Don't know how she did it.
I remember a dessert that was extremely quick to make and magic to eat!

Each guest mixes their own amount of:
A good quality vanilla ice cream
Whipped cream
Coarsely chopped coffee beans
Sprinkle Vodka on top. Lovely!

Right:
Dinner in an unfinished house, but who cares when the food is wonderful and the hostess so charming and gracious?

Below:
A very small and compact garden in the middle of London containing an amazing variety of plants. There are small places in the brick wall to put one's tea cup and biscuits.

# TRADITIONAL ENGLISH TRIFLE FROM KYNANCE MEWS

Kynance mews is by many considered to be the most charming mews in London. A mews is an alley, originally meant for horses, carriages and the servants who worked in the large mansions adjacent (during the Victorian era).

In this picturesque mews, in South Kensington, live inventive cook, Darryll (above) and his partner Andrew. Darryll makes a traditional English trifle dessert, one of the best desserts I have ever eaten. Sweden has wonderful cream tortes with layers of custard (vanilla cream) and fruits and a trifle is similar, but all in a glass bowl. I never forget a good dessert. This one was a winner! (Betty Marsden's was too!)

**TRADITIONAL ENGLISH TRIFLE:**

320 grams trifle sponge (I use 2 packs of trifle sponges)
175 sponge fingers
425g can of pitted black cherries
Raspberry jam
Egg, milk and sugar for approx 300g custard
300 ml double cream
Sherry

METHOD: Slice trifle sponge cakes so that each cake presents the maximum internal surface. Spread jam on one piece and sandwich the two together again. Repeat with all the sponges and then cut them into approximately 2cm x 2 cm squares. Cool.

Drain the cherries but retain the juice. Slice each cherry in half. Fill a trifle bowl with the sponge pieces, the sponge fingers broken into approx 2 cm pieces, and the cherry halves, so that all are spread evenly throughout. Make up the cherry juice with sherry to fill the can to about ¾ full. Pour this over the sponge and cherry mix.

Make the custard by heating the milk, sugar and egg together gently, stirring constantly. When ready pour this over the sponge mixture and allow to cool. It should solidify when cool.

Whip the cream until stiff enough to form peaks and spoon over, spreading it with a fork. You might wish to decorate by grating chocolate over. Ideally, leave in the fridge for several hours before serving.

**Above and left:** Kynance Mews is one of the most sought after, central London properties and wealthy people from all over the world own properties nearby. The once insignificant servants' homes are hugely popular places to live. Some have sumptuous roof terraces. Note the climbing wisteria.

**Left:** The white buildings are the back of the buildings that once were large mansions that now have been converted into flats. The servants lived in the mews houses behind the mansions, and the street entrances to those mews houses were often hidden behind arches to make them less visible to passersby.

# REFLECTIONS

It is important to make buying of food a pleasurable experience. Shopping in a supermarket can unfortunately be a very anonymous affair where there is no time for talk between customers and usually short term workers. But shopping across the counter at a place where you get to know people over a long time, can be very satisfying.

In the tea shop (left) in Gothenburg, you can take your time in asking about and smelling the various teas. Then you can get it all giftwrapped at no extra expense. Plus a lovely smile.

At this local fishmonger (above) they know many of the loyal customers by name and maintain a politeness and customer interest that was common in the past and is welcome, especially today when you, as an individual, are rarely "seen".

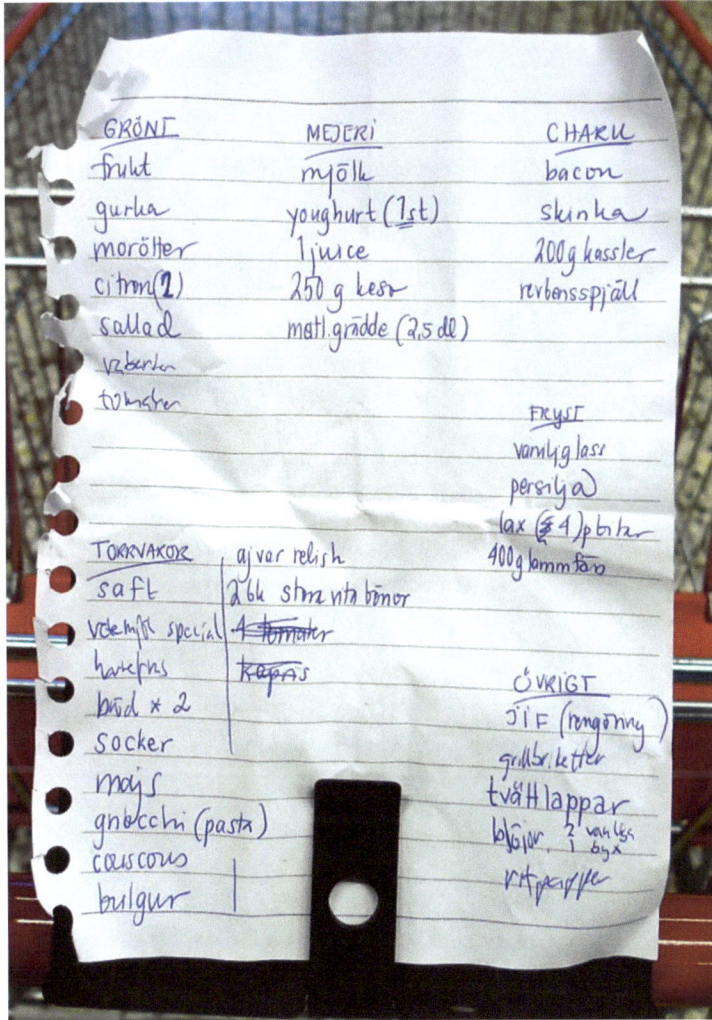

There it was. Staring me in the face, a shopping list on the clip board of the shopping cart I was about to use. The shopping list had obviously been left there by the previous user. But how could one forget such a personal item? And so large?

Then it struck me that it might be fate or some other power giving me a hint to stop being so predictable in my own shopping. Would it not be a kick to discard my own list and use this one already clipped on to the shopping cart? Just for the fun of it -- people are always looking for something new and interesting to make life more exciting; a new tattoo, a larger ring in the nose or maybe some more holes in the jeans.

I could not help admiring this beautifully constructed list, divided up into sections such as: "Greens, Dairy, Meat, Dry goods, Frozen goods, Other." I was impressed and thought about my own list, a messy, not at all well-ordered and scribbled at different times, using pens and pencils of varying colours.

Such an orderly person must surely be very sensible and with sensible food choices. The items on this stranger's shopping list were not objectionable, but I would not buy frozen parsley (there is always fresh) and I would not buy so many smoked meats (not healthy). And no diapers. These were minor objections, the rest I could buy.

So, was I up to the challenge that stared at me from the clip board on the shopping cart? Some people complain that their life is full of lost opportunities. I never wanted to be one of those people. But I have actually been quite daring on many different occasions in my life so I decided that I would stick to my own messy list and would be daring some other time.

**SHOPPING LIST** (translation from Swedish)

| GREENS | DAIRY | MEATS | DRY GOODS | | FROZEN GOODS | OTHER |
|--------|-------|-------|-----------|--|--------------|-------|
| Fruit | Milk | Bacon | Saft (juice type drink) | Gnocchi (pasta) | Vanilla ice cream | JIF cleansing |
| Cucumber | Yoghurt (1) | Ham | Wheat flour, special | Couscous | Parsley | Charcoal |
| Carrotts | I juice | 200 g smoked | Oat crunchies | Bulgar | Salmon (4 pieces) | Diapers |
| Lemons (2) | 250 g. | pork | Bread x 2 | Ajvar relish | Ground lamb (400 g. | Wash cloths |
| Lettuce | Cottage | | Sugar | 2 cans white beans | | Drawing paper |
| ? | Cheese | Ribs | Corn | | | |
| Tomatoes | Cream | | | | | |

# THE BATTLE OF PREPARING A DINNER

Donovan O'Malley

Cooking a meal can be a nightmare if you are not prepared. I once had a nightmare. I was standing by a large stove on a finely clipped lawn in the middle of an English garden. Surrounding me were at least sixty tables with six to eight people at each table, all waiting to be served with food I was expected to cook. I was totally unprepared and no food in sight. I woke up, sweating, relieved that it was only a dream.

In a similarly frustrating dream situation, I thought I had found a way out. I would take frozen bags of spaghetti sauce from the freezer, defrost them quickly and whip up a pasta casserole. But when the frozen bags had been defrosted and I was about to make this emergency casserole the bags were totally empty. Frustration again and again, a relief to wake up.

Some nightmares do exist in real life and there is no escape by waking up. My uncle used to visit some very old and dear university friends in Stockholm every summer. The husband and wife were very intelligent and competent people and she was an excellent cook. My uncle always looked forward to an evening of good food and good conversation. But the years passed and the last summer he met the couple, they had both declined considerably, compared to the previous summer. The husband had recently had a stroke and was not in the best of shape. Sadly the wife had developed an Alzheimers condition so the visit was not at all like the previous visits.

My uncle helped himself to a drink at the bar. When it came time to eat, the wife, an excellent cook announced that "dinner was served" as she had so many other times. But when the roast was brought in and put on the table, it was totally raw, it had never been in the oven.

And that was that. Quite sad.

- 60 -

The Battle of New Orleans by Edward Percy Moran 1910

Preparing a meal is a very intricate process not quite like planning a battle, but there are some similarities. There are a series of practical tasks that have to be thought out in advance, performed according to a timetable and worked out in a parallel fashion to make a number of dishes that have to be baked or chilled just in time for the guests to sit down at the table. Some cooks do all this intuitively. But the brain must be in perfect working order. Drinking and cooking at the same time is not advised or everything might end up upside down (right).

My mother's decline was gradual. It was hard to face the fact that she was not a wonder woman in the kitchen anymore. We should have seen this coming, but we had been too completely spoiled by her managing everything without complaints. Still she had the desire to treat people to a meal. People were expectant as they always had been and wanted to come and visit and the instinct for her was to let them come and she would fix something for them to eat.

But with her limitations she coped by simplifying what she prepared. She pretty much cooked the same uncomplicated dish for every guest, every time. Those were her "last suppers". She kept this up until an incident put her in hospital for a while. After that, other people cooked for her. Her cooking was over.

To my mother and her mother, it was very important to present food on fine linen and lace table cloths with newly polished silver and crystal glasses. It always looked nice with these finely embroidered table cloths, but I always worried that they might get stained with food or red wine -- all that delicate washing needed to get rid of the spots. And ironing. I and many others probably avoid that kind of extra work. But are we too lazy? Have we lost something?

A young relative and his girlfriend had been invited for dinner to a young friend. The guests arrived with hearty appetites, but lo and behold when they found that "the dinner" consisted of pancakes and whipped cream in a spray can.

Nothing else. That was "the dinner".

Obviously the host and their guests had different ideas of what "dinner" meant. To top it off, the spray can of whipped cream was half empty.

A generation ago, we dressed to look nice and perhaps to mark social status (right), but now we have a dress code (jeans with holes in for example) that speaks a different language.

I can do without the lace table cloth. The jeans with the holes are fine if everyone wants to wear the same uniform. But I *definitely* do not want pancakes and spray whipped cream for dinner.

Photo from family archives

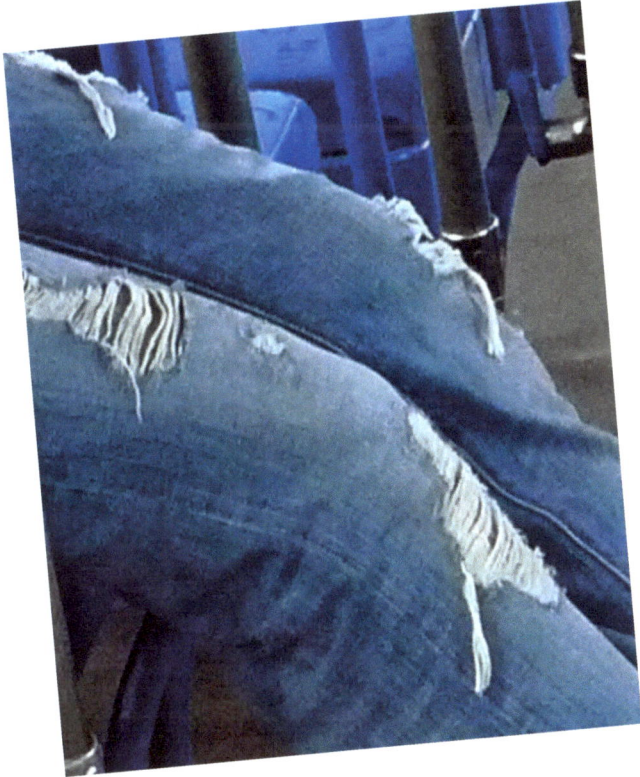

## "EATING OUT"

Once in 1968, on an archipelago trip in Stockholm from the city out to the Drottningholm Palace, on one of their small charming vessels, Donovan and I decided to have a roast beef sandwich from the menu.

A young boy, he could not have been more than eight, went around the small, open tour boat and took orders. We assumed that he must be helping his parents in their business and it seemed charming. Oddly, he asked for payment in advance. Usually people pay for the food after having received it but it was hard to say no to a child who probably only told us what his parents had told him to say.

As I walked around the little boat, I happened to glimpse into the smallish kitchen on board and I saw the little boy working completely alone in the kitchen, no adults in sight. He barely reached up to the counter as he prepared our sandwich. From a plastic bag he took one slice of white bread, buttered it lightly and then took one slice of roast beef from a plastic bag adjacent. No lettuce, no tomato, that was it. Very plain.

He delivered these prepaid and expensive to boot, hardly acceptable or appetizing open face sandwiches. Nobody (us included) protested. We had already paid for them -- and who wants to berate a child of eight?

DONOVAN O'MALLEY

One of the nicest food gifts I ever got was a jar of "Slatko", a rose petal preserve (or rose petal marmalade) from former Yugoslavia. People there make "slatko" (preserves) from the choicest fruits and berries of the year and serve it in a very special way.

When guests arrive, there is the jar of slatko together with a jar of many small spoons. People then take a small spoon and put it in the jar of slatko to sample it. It is quite sweet so a glass of water is offered. The used spoon is discarded and a new one taken for a second taste and so on.

I had often spoken to the young cleaner at my job, who had fled from the war in Yugoslavia and taken a cleaning job in Sweden as so many refugees did in those days. He had a technical education and would obviously move on with further studies. It was interesting to know about the traditions in his homeland and one day he brought me a jar of his mother's slatko. She had sadly not seen him for a long time and wanted him to have something from home.

I was moved to be given one of these jars of delicious rose petal marmalade in which his mother had preserved the sunshine and rose petal fragrance from their country.

A very special gift.

1

**Left and above (1):**
I have never come across an old beater I didn't like - or that I didn't buy. They don't cost much, but I have a fascination with these old mechanical beaters and how they were manufactured.

They have been produced according to the same principles from pressed metal in many different countries. I have seen some made from cast iron too. This one is made in England and has a splatter guard (someone must have come up with this new idea for it is unusual) attached with two rivets. The wooden handles (before plastic) have been turned and painted green. I like the down-to-earth unfussy simplicity. Imagine what a welcome new invention they once were.

My colleagues at work used to berate me for dragging home so much "useless junk" from the flea market across the street from where we worked. I tried explaining that everyone would need one of these mechanical beaters so they can whip cream during a power cut but no, they thought a power cut was a far-fetched possibility and besides, they could live without whipped cream for the duration of a power cut. More importantly, they preferred their modern electric beaters. I use an electric beater too, but I *like* these old charmers.

**Opposite, right and left (2):**
With this elaborate and certainly peculiar looking contraption, you can squeeze your lemon at the table and still maintain your perfect dignity. It must have been very important to some people at one time.

**Opposite centre (3):**
The strange looking (English) sci-fi orange juice press in the centre has a sculptural beauty. It apparently did not catch on as a design since it is not being manufactured anymore.

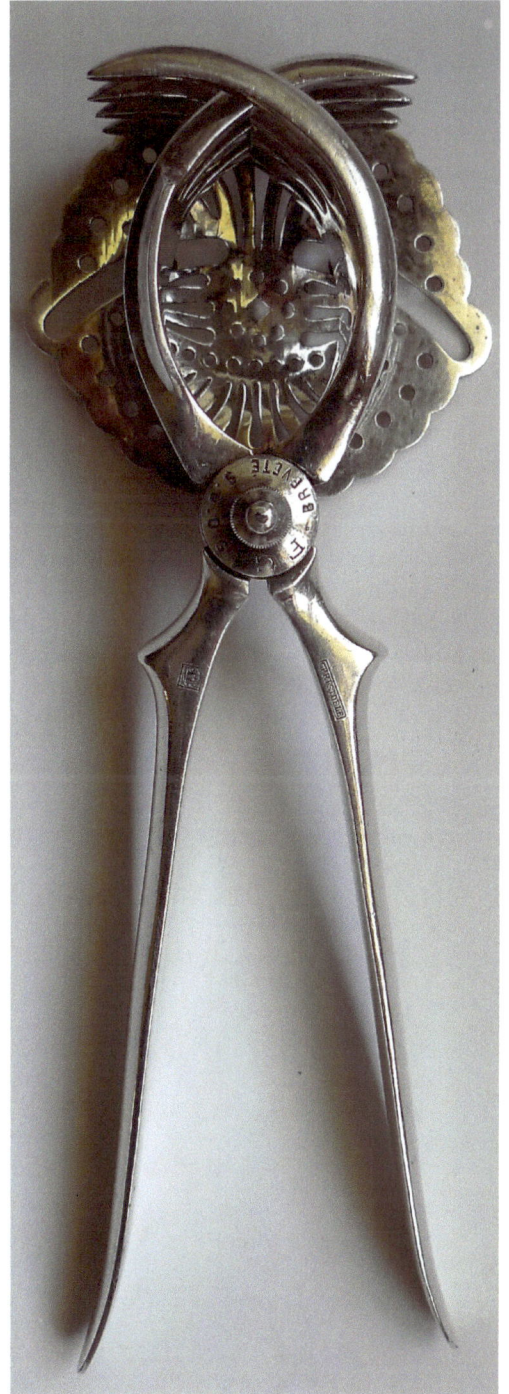

My favourite cook books have become worn and stained with food and shouldn't really be shown to anyone. But they are my old friends. Even if you buy a new edition of a favourite cook book, the recipes you have grown to like might be omitted or altered, so it is best to hold on to the trusted old friends.

Linnéa, my grandmother's fantastic cook never looked in a cook book. She had it all in her head. I myself like to absorb the principle of a dish and then use it like an internal guide and then do my own variations. If you have once made Shepherd's Pie, you can easily use the principle of baking a layer of mashed potatoes over any kind of a moist mix of meat or vegetables (topped with cheese).

In California I was charmed and inspired by Julia Child. She was great fun and I do not forget the time when she had made two variations of coq au vin and when she finished, she took the two lids, clapped them together over her head and said "Voilá!" whilst liquid from the lids dripped over her head - it didn't bother her a bit.

VÅR KOKBOK

1. This is the Swedish comprehensive cookbook "Vår Kokbok" (Our Cook Book) I had in California for six years. It was my education and inspiration.

2. I kept this cook book for sentimental reasons. My grandmother's name is on it and the date 1929. She never cooked except making turkey croquettes of turkey leftovers. Maybe she had some ideas that she would have to cook if the cook was not around. But after 1940, when Linnéa came, she never had to worry anymore.

3. This is a 1926 cook book for housewives and it has a lot of strange, funny and pompous advice for housewives. Also it has many hand painted interesting illustrations (4) this one depicting preserved fruits.

5. In the stack on the right, I might mention Adelle Davis. She was a real health and nutrition guru in the 1970s and I was inspired to grow my own food after reading her.

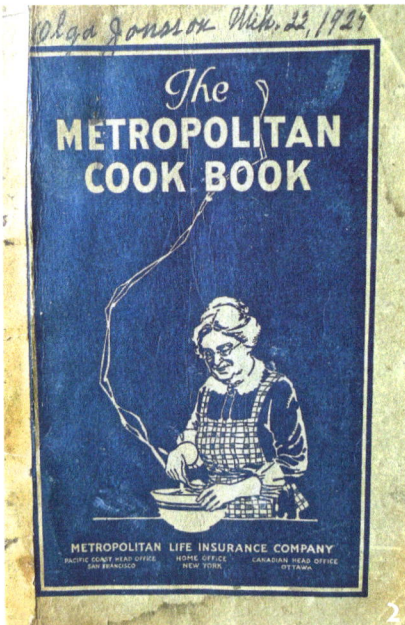

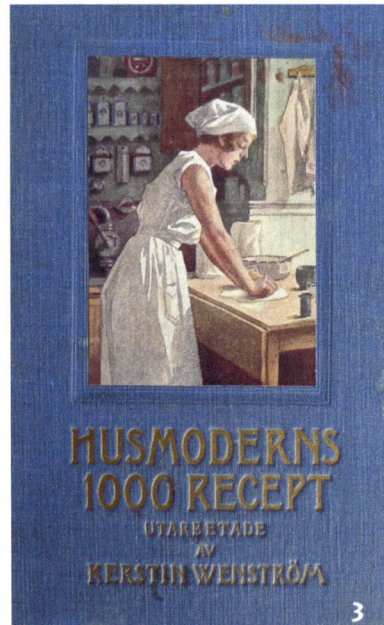

The METROPOLITAN COOK BOOK
METROPOLITAN LIFE INSURANCE COMPANY

HUSMODERNS 1000 RECEPT
UTARBETADE AV KERSTIN WENSTRÖM

1 Bigarråer, 2 Päron, 3 Jordgubbar, 4 Reine-claudes, 5 Hallon.

EVERYDAY FRENCH COOKING    HENRI-PAUL PELLAPRAT    451-W4118-150

Let's Eat Right To Keep Fit    Adelle Davis    451-W4630-150

NEW AMERICAN LIBRARY PUBLISHES SIGNET, SIGNETTE, MENTOR, CLASSIC, PLUME & CAL BOOKS

The French Chef Cookbook    Julia Child    Alfred A. Knopf

THE ZUCCHINI COOKBOOK    •    SIMMONS    $3.50

Joy OF COOKING    Irma S. Rombauer &

THE NEW LAUREL'S KITCHEN

sewood Cookbook    Katzen

ARTIN YAN    QUICK & EASY    CHRONICLE BOOKS    60

5

**GOTHENBURG CLOSEUPS**
**GÖTEBORG NÄRBILDER**
224 photos
(English and Swedish)

**A GARDEN IN GOTHENBURG**
**TRÄDGÅRDSFÖRENINGEN**
132 colour photos
(English and Swedish)

**RESA I TIDEN**
(Swedish essays)

**MY DARLING OLGA**
**Folke Jonsson Letters 1909-1961**
(English)

**THE OLGA & FOLKE**
**PICTURE BOOK**
A Pictorial (140 photos) Companion to
"MY DARLING OLGA"
(English)

**OLGA & FOLKE**
**En bilderbok från en svunnen tid**
(Same as the above in Swedish)

**SKANDALEN OM JIMMY JONES**
Translation into Swedish
by Leif Södergren of
THE JIMMY JONES SKANDAL
A bedtime story for grown-ups
by Donovan O'Malley
Illustrated by the author

www.ingramcontent.com/pod-product-compliance
Lightning Source LLC
Chambersburg PA
CBHW042006080426
42733CB00003B/21